Lightning Focus

Lightning Focus

Matthew Petchinsky

Lightning Focus: Mastering the Art of Productivity in a Distracted World

By: Matthew Petchinsky

Introduction

The Importance of Focus in Modern Life

In today's fast-paced and technology-driven world, focus is one of the most valuable skills we can cultivate. It's not just about productivity; it's about living a life of purpose and clarity. Whether you're striving to achieve career success, build meaningful relationships, or improve your personal well-being, focus acts as the cornerstone for every accomplishment. In its absence, even the most ambitious goals can feel insurmountable, and daily life can devolve into a whirlwind of distractions, leaving us overwhelmed and unfulfilled.

Focus enables us to align our thoughts and actions with our priorities. It gives us the mental bandwidth to solve problems, make informed decisions, and engage deeply in the moments that matter most. In essence, focus is the key to unlocking the potential within us—helping us transform ideas into results, dreams into reality, and fleeting moments into lasting memories.

Yet, despite its importance, maintaining focus has become increasingly difficult in the modern era. Never before in human history have we been bombarded with so much information and so many demands on our attention. From constant notifications on our smartphones to the ceaseless barrage of emails and advertisements, our attention is relentlessly under siege. It's as if the world has declared war on our ability to concentrate, leaving us vulnerable to the subtle yet corrosive effects of distraction.

Why We Struggle with Distractions

Our struggle with distractions is not entirely our fault. Humans are hardwired to respond to novelty. In our evolutionary past, paying attention to sudden changes in the environment—like a rustling in the bushes—could mean the difference between life and death. Today, this same instinct drives us to check our phones at every buzz, scroll endlessly through social media feeds, or switch tasks at the slightest sign of boredom.

Modern technology capitalizes on this innate tendency. Algorithms are designed to keep us engaged for as long as possible, often at the expense of our productivity and well-being. Social media platforms, streaming services, and even workplace tools employ psychological tricks to hijack our attention, leaving us fragmented and perpetually distracted.

But it's not just technology. Our busy lifestyles, endless to-do lists, and the pressure to multitask all contribute to the erosion of our focus. Instead of feeling accomplished at the end of the day, we're left wondering where the time went, frustrated by how little we actually achieved. This cycle of distraction not only undermines our effectiveness but also chips away at our self-esteem and mental health.

How This Book Will Help

This book is your guide to reclaiming control over your attention in a world that profits from distraction. It offers practical, actionable strategies to help you cultivate laser-sharp focus, no matter your circumstances. From understanding the psychology of attention to creating environments that support deep work, each chapter is designed to empower you with the tools you need to cut through the noise and achieve your goals.

We'll explore why focus is so elusive and uncover the habits, mindsets, and techniques that can help you stay on track. You'll learn how to identify and eliminate distractions, set clear priorities, and create a personal roadmap for sustained productivity and fulfillment. Whether you're a professional juggling deadlines, a student aiming for academic success, or simply someone looking to regain control over their life, this book will provide you with a blueprint for thriving in an age of endless distractions.

Ultimately, focus is not just a skill—it's a discipline, a mindset, and a way of life. By mastering it, you can unlock your potential and live with greater clarity, intention, and purpose. Let's embark on this journey together to transform your relationship with focus and help you create the life you truly desire.

Chapter 1: The Science of Focus

Focus is often seen as a skill, but at its core, it's a mental state governed by the complex workings of your brain. Understanding how your brain processes information, manages distractions, and responds to stimuli is crucial for developing the ability to concentrate deeply and effectively. In this chapter, we'll explore the science of focus and uncover practical insights into how your brain functions. We'll also help you identify your personal attention triggers, empowering you to take the first step toward mastering your focus.

How Your Brain Works and Reacts to Distractions

To understand focus, we first need to examine how the brain operates. At any given moment, your brain is bombarded with sensory input—sounds, sights, smells, and even internal thoughts and emotions. To function effectively, your brain must filter out the noise and prioritize what truly matters. This process primarily occurs in the **prefrontal cortex**, the area of the brain responsible for decision-making, attention, and goal-setting.

The Role of the Prefrontal Cortex

The prefrontal cortex acts as your brain's CEO, making decisions about where to direct your attention and energy. When you're deeply focused on a task, this part of your brain is actively suppressing irrelevant distractions and enhancing the neural pathways required for sustained concentration. However, the prefrontal cortex has its limits. It can only manage a certain amount of information at once, which is why multitasking often leads to reduced efficiency and errors.

The Impact of Dopamine

Dopamine, often called the "reward chemical," plays a significant role in focus and distraction. Each time you complete a task or experience something novel, your brain releases a burst of dopamine, reinforcing the behavior. This is why distractions, especially those involving technology, can be so addictive. Scrolling through social media, checking notifications, or watching videos provides instant gratification in the form of dopamine hits, pulling your attention away from more meaningful activities.

The Default Mode Network

When you're not actively focusing, your brain switches to its **default mode network (DMN)**. This network is responsible for daydreaming, reflecting, and mind-wandering. While the DMN can be valuable for creative thinking, it often leads to unintentional distractions when you're trying to concentrate. Understanding the DMN's role can help you identify when your mind starts to drift and take steps to refocus.

Why Distractions Are So Powerful

Distractions exploit your brain's natural tendencies. For example:

1. **Novelty Bias**: Your brain is hardwired to seek out new and interesting information. This evolutionary trait once helped humans detect threats but now drives the compulsion to check emails or click on every notification.
2. **Limited Attention Span**: The human attention span is finite. Studies suggest that prolonged focus without breaks can lead to mental fatigue, making it harder to resist distractions.
3. **Stress and Anxiety**: High levels of stress or anxiety can over-activate the brain's emotional centers, such as the amygdala, pulling focus away from rational thought and productive tasks.

By understanding these mechanisms, you can begin to counteract the forces that pull you away from focus.

Identifying Your Personal Attention Triggers

While external distractions are everywhere, many of the interruptions to your focus originate from within. These internal distractions, known as **attention triggers**, vary from person to person. Identifying yours is a critical step toward mastering your focus.

Common Attention Triggers

1. **Technological Interruptions**: Notifications, buzzing phones, and pop-up alerts are among the most pervasive distractions in modern life. These external triggers can quickly derail even the most disciplined mind.

2. **Emotional Distractions**: Stress, anxiety, and unresolved emotions often cause your thoughts to wander. For example, worrying about a deadline can prevent you from focusing on the work needed to meet it.

3. **Physical Triggers**: Hunger, fatigue, or discomfort can significantly impair your ability to concentrate. A growling stomach or an uncomfortable chair might seem minor, but they compete for your attention nonetheless.

4. **Environmental Factors**: Noise, clutter, or other distractions in your workspace can make it difficult to concentrate.

5. **Mental Habits**: A tendency to procrastinate, perfectionism, or habitual multitasking can lead to self-sabotage when trying to focus.

Steps to Identify Your Triggers

1. **Self-Observation**: Start by observing your behavior during periods of focus. What external or internal factors most often disrupt your concentration? Keep a journal to track these moments.
2. **Environmental Audit**: Examine your workspace. Is it conducive to deep work? Note any distractions, such as noise, clutter, or frequent interruptions.
3. **Analyze Patterns**: Review your daily routine. Are there specific times when you're more prone to distractions? Do you notice a decline in focus after eating certain foods or during certain activities?
4. **Emotional Awareness**: Pay attention to your emotional state. Are you more likely to be distracted when you're anxious, bored, or overwhelmed? Emotional triggers can be subtle but powerful.
5. **Technology Usage**: Monitor how often you reach for your phone or get sidetracked by digital notifications. Apps that track screen time can provide valuable insights.

Developing Awareness

Once you've identified your triggers, the next step is to cultivate awareness. When you recognize a trigger in real-time, you gain the power to interrupt the cycle of distraction. For example:

- If a notification pops up, pause and decide whether it truly requires immediate attention.
- If you notice your mind wandering, gently guide your focus back to the task at hand without judgment.

Conclusion: Building a Foundation for Focus

Understanding how your brain works and recognizing your attention triggers are essential building blocks for mastering focus. The brain's susceptibility to distraction isn't a weakness—it's simply a trait that can be managed with the right strategies. By becoming aware of how distractions arise, both externally and internally, you can start to take proactive steps to reclaim your attention.

The science of focus isn't just about knowing how the brain functions; it's about using that knowledge to make intentional choices. With this foundation, you're now ready to explore practical techniques and habits that will empower you to take control of your focus and achieve your goals.

Chapter 2: Decluttering Your Mental Space

In a world where information is abundant and demands are constant, the ability to declutter your mental space is crucial for achieving sustained focus. Mental overload doesn't just sap your energy—it creates a chaotic inner environment where productivity, creativity, and decision-making are stifled. In this chapter, we'll explore simple, effective techniques to eliminate mental overload and guide you through the process of creating a distraction-free environment that supports deep focus and clarity.

Simple Techniques to Eliminate Mental Overload

Mental overload happens when your brain is trying to process too many thoughts, tasks, and worries at once. Just as a cluttered desk can make it hard to find what you need, a cluttered mind can leave you feeling overwhelmed and directionless. The following techniques are designed to help you clear the mental clutter and create space for what truly matters.

1. Practice Mind Dumping

Mind dumping is the act of transferring all your thoughts, worries, and to-dos onto paper or a digital document. This technique reduces cognitive load by freeing your brain from the effort of holding onto everything at once.

How to do it:

- Set aside 10–15 minutes at the start or end of your day.
- Write down everything that's on your mind—tasks, ideas, worries, and reminders—without filtering or organizing.
- Once you've completed the dump, review the list and categorize items into actionable tasks, long-term goals, or things to let go of.

This practice not only clears your mental space but also provides clarity on what needs your attention.

2. Prioritize and Simplify

Not all tasks are created equal, and attempting to tackle everything at once leads to burnout. Prioritization helps you focus on what truly matters.

Steps to prioritize effectively:

1. **Use the Eisenhower Matrix:**
   - Categorize tasks into four quadrants:
     - *Urgent and Important*: Do these immediately.
     - *Important but Not Urgent*: Schedule these for later.
     - *Urgent but Not Important*: Delegate these if possible.
     - *Neither Urgent nor Important*: Eliminate these.
2. **Adopt the "Rule of Three":**
   - Identify three key tasks to accomplish each day. This keeps your to-do list manageable and your focus sharp.
3. **Eliminate the Nonessential:**
   - Ask yourself: *Does this truly align with my goals?* Let go of tasks or commitments that don't add value to your life.

3. Embrace Single-Tasking

Multitasking is often glorified, but it's one of the biggest culprits of mental overload. Switching between tasks fragments your attention and drains your mental energy.

How to single-task:

- Dedicate specific time blocks to individual tasks.
- Remove all distractions (e.g., turn off notifications, close unnecessary tabs).
- Use a timer (like the Pomodoro Technique) to stay focused for a set period, followed by short breaks.

4. Cultivate Mindfulness

Mindfulness is the practice of staying present in the moment, which can help you avoid being overwhelmed by racing thoughts.

Practical mindfulness exercises:

- **Breath Awareness**: Spend 2–3 minutes focusing on your breath. Inhale deeply, exhale slowly, and anchor your attention to the rhythm of your breathing.
- **Mindful Breaks**: Take short breaks during the day to ground yourself. Look out a window, stretch, or enjoy a few moments of silence.
- **Body Scan**: Close your eyes and mentally scan your body, starting from your head and moving to your toes. Notice any tension and consciously relax those areas.

5. Use Technology Wisely

While technology can be a source of distraction, it can also be leveraged to help manage mental overload.

Tips for smarter tech use:

- Use productivity apps like Trello, Notion, or Todoist to organize tasks and projects.
- Set screen time limits on your devices to reduce time spent on nonproductive activities.
- Turn on "Do Not Disturb" mode during work sessions to minimize interruptions.

Creating a Distraction-Free Environment

Your external environment plays a significant role in shaping your ability to focus. By designing a space that minimizes distractions, you create a physical foundation for mental clarity.

1. Optimize Your Workspace

A cluttered workspace leads to a cluttered mind. Simplify and organize your surroundings to eliminate unnecessary visual and physical distractions.

Steps to declutter your workspace:

- **Clear the Surface**: Keep only the essentials on your desk (e.g., laptop, notebook, and a water bottle).
- **Organize Tools**: Use storage solutions like drawers, trays, or containers to keep supplies out of sight but accessible.
- **Add Personal Touches**: Include a plant, a motivational quote, or a calming object to make the space inviting without overloading it.

2. Manage Noise Levels

Noise is a common distraction, especially in shared or open spaces. Controlling your auditory environment can significantly improve focus.

Solutions for noise management:

- Use noise-canceling headphones or earplugs.
- Play background music or white noise to mask distracting sounds.
- Designate a quiet zone for deep work, if possible.

3. Control Digital Distractions

Digital devices are among the most persistent sources of distraction. Setting boundaries around their use is essential for focus.

Strategies to control digital distractions:

- **Set App Limits**: Use features like app timers to restrict usage of social media or entertainment apps.
- **Use Focus Tools**: Install browser extensions like Freedom or StayFocusd to block distracting websites during work hours.
- **Create a Phone-Free Zone**: Keep your phone out of reach or in another room while working.

4. Simplify Your Visual Environment

Visual clutter can unconsciously drain your attention. A clean and organized space helps your brain stay focused.

Tips for simplifying visuals:

- Use neutral or calming colors in your workspace.
- Limit the number of items on walls or bulletin boards to avoid overstimulation.
- Keep your desktop (both physical and digital) tidy by organizing files and removing unnecessary icons.

5. Establish Rituals for Focus

Rituals signal to your brain that it's time to transition into a state of focus. These can help you mentally and physically prepare for deep work.

Examples of focus rituals:

- Start your work session with 5 minutes of meditation or journaling.
- Light a candle or use an essential oil diffuser with a calming scent.
- Play a specific playlist or ambient sound that you associate with productivity.

Conclusion: The Foundation of Mental Clarity

Decluttering your mental space and creating a distraction-free environment are foundational steps toward achieving sustained focus. By addressing both internal and external sources of distraction, you can create the conditions necessary for deep work and mental clarity. These strategies aren't just about removing what's unnecessary—they're about making intentional choices that align with your goals and values.

With a clear mind and a supportive environment, you'll find it easier to prioritize, concentrate, and accomplish what truly matters.

Chapter 3: Building the Focus Habit

Focus is not a trait you either have or don't have—it's a skill that can be strengthened with consistent practice. Much like a muscle, your ability to focus grows stronger the more you use it intentionally. Developing the habit of focus requires commitment, deliberate effort, and a structured approach to embedding it into your daily routine. In this chapter, we'll explore practical, daily practices to strengthen your focus and show you how to leverage micro-habits for lasting productivity.

Daily Practices to Strengthen Your Focus Muscle

The key to strengthening your focus is regular practice. By incorporating focus-building exercises into your daily routine, you can train your brain to resist distractions and sustain attention for longer periods.

1. Start with Morning Intentions

How you begin your day sets the tone for everything that follows. Starting your morning with clear intentions primes your mind for focus and productivity.

How to set morning intentions:

- Spend 5–10 minutes in the morning identifying your top priorities for the day. Write them down to create a mental roadmap.
- Visualize yourself completing these tasks successfully, focusing on how you'll feel afterward.
- Avoid reaching for your phone or checking emails first thing in the morning to prevent reactive thinking.

This simple practice helps your brain prioritize and commit to meaningful tasks instead of succumbing to distractions.

2. Schedule Deep Work Sessions

Deep work is the ability to focus without distraction on cognitively demanding tasks. Scheduling dedicated time for deep work allows you to maximize productivity and create flow states.

Steps to implement deep work:

- Identify the most mentally demanding task of your day and allocate a time block for it.
- Choose a distraction-free environment for your session (refer to Chapter 2 for tips).
- Use tools like the **Pomodoro Technique**: Work in 25-minute intervals with 5-minute breaks, gradually increasing the duration as your focus improves.
- Make deep work a non-negotiable part of your daily routine.

3. Practice Focused Meditation

Meditation isn't just about relaxation—it's a powerful tool for training your attention. By practicing focused meditation, you can enhance your brain's ability to sustain focus over time.

How to practice focused meditation:

- Find a quiet space and sit comfortably.
- Choose an anchor for your attention, such as your breath, a word, or an object.
- Whenever your mind starts to wander, gently guide it back to your anchor without judgment.

Start with 5 minutes a day and gradually increase the duration as your mental endurance grows.

4. Prioritize Physical and Mental Health

Your brain's ability to focus is closely tied to your overall well-being. Poor sleep, an unhealthy diet, and lack of exercise can all impair your attention span.

Daily health practices for better focus:

- **Sleep**: Aim for 7–9 hours of quality sleep each night to support cognitive function.
- **Diet**: Fuel your brain with nutrient-rich foods, including omega-3s (found in fish), antioxidants (from fruits and vegetables), and healthy fats (like avocados and nuts).
- **Exercise**: Engage in at least 30 minutes of physical activity daily. Exercise increases blood flow to the brain, boosting concentration and mood.

5. Journal for Mental Clarity

Journaling is a simple yet effective way to process thoughts, eliminate mental clutter, and maintain focus.

How to incorporate journaling:

- At the end of each day, reflect on your achievements, challenges, and areas for improvement.
- Use your journal to track progress on focus-building goals and identify patterns in your distractions.

Journaling serves as both a mental reset and a way to stay accountable to your focus practice.

Leveraging Micro-Habits for Lasting Productivity

While daily practices lay the foundation for focus, micro-habits can make the process sustainable. Micro-habits are small, manageable actions that require minimal effort but yield significant results when practiced consistently.

1. The Power of Small Wins

Micro-habits work by creating momentum through small, achievable victories. These wins build confidence and reinforce the habit loop.

Examples of micro-habits for focus:

- Start your work session by taking three deep breaths to center yourself.
- Set a timer for 5 minutes of uninterrupted focus on a task. Gradually increase the duration over time.
- Begin each deep work session by clearing your workspace for 30 seconds.

These seemingly minor actions compound over time, creating lasting changes in your ability to focus.

2. Habit Stacking

Habit stacking is a technique where you pair a new habit with an existing one. This approach leverages the consistency of your current routines to build new behaviors.

How to stack focus habits:

- After brushing your teeth in the morning, spend 2 minutes setting your priorities for the day.
- Before starting lunch, review your morning progress and adjust your afternoon tasks.

- At the end of the day, write down one thing you'll focus on tomorrow.

By attaching focus habits to familiar routines, you'll integrate them seamlessly into your daily life.

3. The Two-Minute Rule

The Two-Minute Rule is a productivity technique that helps you overcome resistance to starting tasks. The idea is to commit to just two minutes of a task, reducing the psychological barrier to getting started.

How to apply the rule:

- When you're struggling to focus, tell yourself you'll work on the task for just two minutes.
- Often, this small action is enough to build momentum and carry you into a flow state.

4. Reward and Reinforce

Positive reinforcement is a powerful motivator for building new habits. By rewarding yourself for maintaining focus, you create a feedback loop that encourages consistency.

Ideas for rewards:

- Take a short walk or enjoy a healthy snack after completing a focus session.
- Allow yourself 10 minutes of leisure activity (e.g., scrolling social media or watching a video) after finishing a major task.
- Celebrate your weekly progress with a more significant treat, like a favorite meal or a relaxing activity.

5. Automate Decision-Making

Decision fatigue can drain your focus before you even begin your work. Simplifying repetitive decisions frees up mental energy for more important tasks.

How to reduce decision fatigue:

- Plan your day the night before, outlining your top priorities and schedule.
- Create a capsule wardrobe or meal plan to eliminate choices about what to wear or eat.
- Use templates or standard workflows for recurring tasks.

Automation allows you to conserve your focus for where it matters most.

Conclusion: Focus as a Lifelong Practice

Building the focus habit is not a one-time effort; it's a lifelong practice that evolves as you grow. By incorporating daily practices and leveraging micro-habits, you can gradually transform focus from a fleeting state into a reliable skill. Remember, progress is made one small step at a time, and consistency is far more important than perfection.

With a solid foundation in focus habits, you'll find yourself better equipped to handle challenges, achieve goals, and maintain clarity in the face of distractions.

Chapter 4: Time Blocking Like a Pro

Time is your most valuable resource, and the way you manage it determines your success, productivity, and overall satisfaction in life. Time blocking is one of the most effective methods for taking control of your schedule, ensuring that you allocate dedicated periods for deep work, creative flow, and essential tasks. In this chapter, we'll dive into how you can master time blocking to maximize your productivity and achieve your goals. We'll also explore tools and techniques to enhance your time management skills and make this system work seamlessly for you.

Scheduling for Deep Work and Creative Flow

Time blocking is the practice of dividing your day into blocks of time, each dedicated to specific tasks or activities. By assigning every minute a purpose, you eliminate the uncertainty of deciding what to do next and protect your focus from distractions. When applied correctly, time blocking helps you schedule periods for deep work and creative flow—two critical states for productivity and innovation.

1. Understanding Deep Work and Creative Flow

- **Deep Work**: Coined by productivity expert Cal Newport, deep work refers to the ability to focus without distraction on cognitively demanding tasks. This state is essential for producing high-quality work and solving complex problems.
- **Creative Flow**: Flow is a state of complete immersion in an activity where time seems to disappear, and your mind is fully engaged. Achieving flow is particularly important for tasks requiring creativity, such as writing, designing, or brainstorming.

Both states demand uninterrupted focus, making time blocking an ideal strategy for creating the conditions necessary to access them.

2. Designing a Time Block Schedule for Maximum Focus

1. **Identify Your Peak Productivity Hours**:
   Everyone has a unique rhythm of energy and focus throughout the day. Some people are most alert in the morning, while others thrive in the afternoon or evening. Schedule your deep work and creative flow blocks during these peak hours.

2. **Group Similar Tasks Together**:
   Avoid switching between different types of tasks, as context switching drains your mental energy. For example, schedule all administrative work (emails, calls, scheduling) in one block and reserve another for strategic or creative tasks.

3. **Break Your Day into Purposeful Blocks**:
   - **Morning Block**: Prioritize deep work on high-impact tasks.
   - **Midday Block**: Allocate time for meetings, collaborative work, or low-energy tasks.
   - **Afternoon/Evening Block**: Focus on creative or routine tasks that require less mental intensity.

4. **Schedule Breaks**:
   Work breaks into your time blocks to prevent burnout and maintain focus. A 5–10 minute break after every 25–50 minutes of work (as in the Pomodoro Technique) or a longer break after extended focus periods works well.

5. **Protect Your Time**:
   Treat your time blocks as sacred. Communicate with colleagues, family, or friends about your schedule, and use tools like "Do Not Disturb" mode on your devices to minimize interruptions.

3. Integrating Flexibility into Time Blocking

While time blocking is highly structured, life is unpredictable, and flexibility is key to long-term success.

- **Plan for the Unexpected**: Allocate buffer time in your schedule for unplanned tasks, interruptions, or overruns.
- **Review and Adjust**: At the end of each day, assess whether your time blocks worked as planned. Adjust your schedule for the following day based on what you learn.
- **Use Overlapping Blocks**: For projects with uncertain durations, use overlapping blocks with a priority hierarchy. For example, if you finish Task A early, move on to Task B without delay.

Tools and Techniques for Effective Time Management

Mastering time blocking requires the right tools and techniques. These resources help you organize your schedule, track progress, and stay accountable to your goals.

Digital Tools for Time Blocking

1. **Google Calendar**:

   Google Calendar is one of the most popular tools for time blocking. You can create color-coded events, set reminders, and sync your schedule across devices.

Pro Tip: Use different colors for categories like deep work, meetings, and personal time to visualize your priorities at a glance.

2.Notion:

Notion combines task management, note-taking, and calendar functionality, making it an excellent tool for creating customizable time block schedules.

Pro Tip: Use Notion templates to create recurring blocks for weekly or daily routines.

3.Trello or Asana:

These project management tools help you organize tasks by priority and assign them to specific time blocks in your day.

Pro Tip: Pair Trello or Asana with a digital calendar to ensure your tasks align with your time-blocked schedule.

4.Focus Apps:

Apps like Forest, Focus@Will, or Freedom help you stay on track by limiting distractions and creating a conducive environment for deep work.

2. Analog Techniques for Time Blocking

1. **The Bullet Journal Method**:

   Use a bullet journal to map out your daily schedule. Writing your blocks by hand can help you internalize your plan and commit to it.

Pro Tip: Create a simple grid or timeline to visually segment your day into blocks.

1. **The Time Blocking Planner**:

   Invest in a dedicated planner designed specifically for time blocking. These planners often include pre-drawn grids or columns to make scheduling easier.

3. Advanced Time Blocking Techniques

1. **Time Batching**:
   Group similar tasks into a single block to minimize context switching. For example, schedule all emails, calls, and administrative work in one block rather than scattering them throughout the day.
2. **Task Chunking**:
   Break large, complex projects into smaller, manageable chunks and assign each chunk to its own time block. This reduces overwhelm and helps you track progress.
3. **Energy Matching**:
   Align your time blocks with your energy levels throughout the day. Save high-energy blocks for challenging tasks and low-energy blocks for simpler ones.
4. **Reverse Time Blocking**:
   Instead of planning your day from the start, begin with the end in mind. Block time for your long-term goals and priorities first, then fit smaller tasks around them.
5. **Accountability Pairing**:
   Share your time block schedule with an accountability partner. This external layer of commitment increases the likelihood of sticking to your plan.

Conclusion: The Power of Intentional Time Management

Time blocking isn't just about scheduling—it's about taking control of your time to align your actions with your goals. By mastering the art of time blocking, you can create a balance between deep work and creative flow, ensuring that your most important tasks receive the focus they deserve.

The tools and techniques discussed in this chapter provide the foundation for effective time management, but their success depends on consistency and adaptability. As you implement time blocking in your life, remember that it's a dynamic process. Experiment, refine, and adjust your approach to fit your unique needs and circumstances.

Chapter 5: The Long-Term Focus Formula

Focus is not a temporary state—it's a lifelong discipline that evolves with you. The ability to maintain focus for years, even decades, is the cornerstone of sustained success. However, life is full of changes, challenges, and unexpected twists that can disrupt even the most disciplined habits. The key lies in developing a long-term focus formula: a system that not only supports your current goals but also adapts to your evolving priorities.

In this chapter, we'll explore strategies for maintaining focus over the long haul and how to adapt your focus to navigate new challenges without losing clarity.

Maintaining Focus for a Lifetime of Success

Long-term focus requires more than a single set of habits—it demands a mindset and lifestyle designed to reinforce clarity, purpose, and resilience over time.

1. Build a Strong "Why"

Sustained focus is rooted in a clear sense of purpose. When you know why you're doing something, it becomes easier to stay committed, even when distractions arise.

How to discover your "why":

- Reflect on your core values and long-term goals. What truly matters to you?
- Visualize the future you want to create. How does staying focused today contribute to that vision?
- Write down your mission statement. Keep it somewhere visible to remind yourself of your purpose.

Example: If your goal is to build a successful business, your "why" might be to provide financial security for your family or to create something meaningful for your community.

2. Develop a Resilient Mindset

Life will inevitably test your focus with setbacks, failures, and distractions. Building mental resilience allows you to stay on track despite challenges.

Steps to cultivate resilience:

1. **Reframe Failure:** View setbacks as opportunities to learn and grow, not as reasons to give up.
2. **Practice Gratitude:** Regularly acknowledge the progress you've made and the resources you have. This fosters a positive mindset.
3. **Strengthen Self-Discipline:** Treat your commitments to focus as non-negotiable. The more you stick to your habits, the stronger your self-discipline becomes.

3. Create Systems, Not Just Goals

Goals are important, but systems—the routines and processes you follow daily—are what keep you moving forward consistently.

How to build focus-supporting systems:

- **Automate Repetitive Decisions:** Streamline your day by creating default choices for meals, clothing, and routines to conserve mental energy for meaningful tasks.
- **Review and Reflect Regularly:** Schedule weekly or monthly reviews to assess your progress and adjust your approach.
- **Set Milestones:** Break long-term goals into smaller milestones to stay motivated and track success incrementally.

4. Keep Your Mind and Body in Peak Condition

Sustaining focus for a lifetime requires taking care of your physical and mental health. A healthy mind and body are your foundation for enduring success.

Essential practices:

- **Exercise Regularly:** Physical activity improves brain function, reduces stress, and enhances focus.
- **Prioritize Sleep:** Consistent, high-quality sleep is crucial for maintaining cognitive performance.
- **Lifelong Learning:** Keep your mind sharp by reading, taking courses, or exploring new hobbies.

5. Celebrate Small Wins

Acknowledging progress, no matter how small, reinforces positive habits and keeps you motivated.

Ways to celebrate progress:

- Treat yourself to something you enjoy after completing a major milestone.
- Share your achievements with friends or an accountability partner.
- Reflect on how far you've come and how much closer you are to your goals.

Adapting to New Challenges Without Losing Clarity

The ability to adapt your focus to new challenges and priorities is critical in a world that's constantly changing. Without flexibility, you risk becoming stuck in outdated routines or overwhelmed by shifting demands.

1. Embrace the Power of Re-Evaluation

As your goals evolve, so should your focus strategies. Periodically reassess your priorities to ensure alignment with your current circumstances and ambitions.

How to re-evaluate effectively:

- **Conduct a Quarterly Check-In:** Ask yourself what's working, what's not, and what needs to change.
- **Revisit Your "Why":** Does your purpose still resonate, or has it shifted?
- **Update Your Systems:** Refine your routines and tools to match your new goals.

2. Stay Agile in the Face of Change

Flexibility doesn't mean abandoning focus; it means adjusting your approach to stay aligned with your objectives.

Tips for staying agile:

- **Adopt a Growth Mindset:** View change as an opportunity to learn and grow, rather than a disruption.
- **Set Short-Term Goals:** When faced with uncertainty, focus on immediate, actionable steps to maintain momentum.

- **Experiment and Iterate:** Try new strategies or tools to find what works best in your current situation.

3. Manage Stress and Uncertainty

Stress and uncertainty can derail focus, especially during times of upheaval. Developing coping mechanisms helps you stay grounded and clear-headed.

Stress management strategies:

- **Practice Mindfulness:** Regular meditation or deep breathing exercises can calm your mind and improve focus.
- **Maintain a Support Network:** Surround yourself with people who encourage and support your goals.
- **Set Boundaries:** Protect your focus by saying no to distractions or commitments that don't align with your priorities.

4. Plan for the Long Game

Adapting to challenges often requires balancing short-term demands with long-term aspirations.

How to balance short-term and long-term focus:

- **Use the 80/20 Rule:** Focus 80% of your time on activities that directly contribute to your long-term goals, while reserving 20% for urgent short-term tasks.
- **Create a Vision Board:** Visualize your long-term goals to keep them top of mind, even when tackling immediate challenges.
- **Invest in Skills:** Focus on developing skills that will serve you in the long term, such as communication, leadership, or problem-solving.

5. Anticipate and Prepare for Setbacks

No journey is without obstacles. Preparing for setbacks ensures that they don't derail your focus permanently.

How to prepare for setbacks:

- **Identify Potential Risks:** What challenges are most likely to arise in your journey?
- **Have Contingency Plans:** Develop backup strategies for staying on track when faced with obstacles.
- **Stay Positive:** Remember that setbacks are temporary and don't define your ability to succeed.

Conclusion: Focus as a Lifelong Compass

The long-term focus formula isn't about rigid discipline—it's about creating a sustainable, flexible approach that supports your evolving goals and ambitions. By maintaining clarity on your purpose, building resilient systems, and adapting to new challenges, you can ensure that focus becomes a lifelong compass guiding you toward success.

Appendix A: Recommended Tools, Apps, and Resources for Improving Focus

Achieving and sustaining focus requires the right support system. In today's digital age, a wide variety of tools and resources are available to help you stay organized, minimize distractions, and maximize productivity. This appendix provides a comprehensive list of the most effective tools, apps, and resources for improving focus across different areas of life.

1. Tools for Time Management

Effective time management is the foundation of focus. The following tools help you plan your day, prioritize tasks, and make the most of your time.

Digital Calendars

- **Google Calendar**: A versatile and user-friendly calendar that allows you to schedule tasks, set reminders, and integrate with other apps. Color-coded events make it easy to distinguish between work, personal time, and deep focus sessions.
- **Microsoft Outlook Calendar**: Ideal for those using Microsoft Office, this calendar integrates seamlessly with email and task management tools.
- **Fantastical**: A premium calendar app with an intuitive design, natural language input for scheduling, and robust task management features.

Task Management Apps

- **Todoist**: A powerful task management app that helps you organize tasks into projects, set deadlines, and create recurring reminders.
- **Trello**: A visually intuitive app that uses boards and cards to organize tasks. Perfect for those who prefer a more visual approach to project management.
- **Asana**: A project management tool ideal for teams or individuals who need to break tasks into subtasks and track progress over time.

2. Tools for Minimizing Distractions

Staying focused often means reducing or eliminating distractions. These tools can help block interruptions and create a distraction-free environment.

Website and App Blockers

- **Freedom**: Blocks distracting websites and apps across all devices, allowing you to focus on your work without temptation.
- **StayFocusd**: A browser extension for Chrome that limits the amount of time you can spend on distracting websites.
- **Cold Turkey**: A distraction-blocking app with robust scheduling features, allowing you to lock yourself out of distractions for predefined periods.

Focus-Friendly Apps

- **Forest**: Gamifies focus by growing virtual trees as you stay off your phone. Great for building focus habits in a fun and visual way.
- **Focus@Will**: Plays scientifically optimized music to improve concentration and maintain attention.

- **Brain.fm**: Uses AI-generated music designed to enhance focus, relaxation, or sleep.

3. Tools for Managing Information Overload

Information overload is a common cause of mental clutter. These tools help you manage and organize information more effectively.

Note-Taking and Knowledge Management

- **Evernote**: A robust tool for capturing and organizing notes, to-do lists, and ideas in one place.
- **Notion**: Combines note-taking, project management, and task tracking into a single, customizable workspace.
- **Roam Research**: A knowledge management app designed for interconnected note-taking, ideal for brainstorming and idea mapping.

Read-It-Later Apps

- **Pocket**: Save articles, videos, and other content to read later, allowing you to avoid distractions while still capturing valuable resources.
- **Instapaper**: Similar to Pocket, Instapaper lets you save and organize content for focused reading sessions.

4. Tools for Enhancing Mental and Physical Well-Being

Your mental and physical health significantly impact your ability to focus. The following tools support mindfulness, stress management, and overall well-being.

Meditation and Mindfulness Apps

- **Headspace**: Offers guided meditations, mindfulness exercises, and sleep aids to improve mental clarity and focus.
- **Calm**: Focuses on meditation, sleep stories, and breathing exercises to reduce stress and improve concentration.
- **Insight Timer**: A free app with thousands of guided meditations and a timer for self-directed meditation.

Exercise and Movement

- **Seven – 7 Minute Workout**: Provides quick, guided workouts to help you maintain physical health without a significant time commitment.
- **Yoga with Adriene (YouTube)**: A free resource for yoga routines that combine physical movement with mindfulness.
- **Strava**: Tracks physical activities like running or cycling, helping you stay active and energized for better focus.

5. Tools for Focused Learning and Skill Development

Lifelong learning keeps your brain sharp and enhances focus. These tools are excellent for acquiring new skills or knowledge while maintaining concentration.

- **Duolingo**: A gamified language-learning app that encourages daily practice and sustained focus.
- **Khan Academy**: A free platform offering courses in various subjects, from math to art history, designed for focused learning.
- **Coursera**: Provides access to online courses from top universities, allowing you to learn in a structured and distraction-free environment.

6. Tools for Creating Focus-Friendly Environments

Your environment has a significant impact on your ability to concentrate. These tools help you optimize your surroundings for better focus.

Noise-Canceling Headphones

- **Bose QuietComfort Series**: Renowned for their superior noise-canceling capabilities, these headphones create a distraction-free auditory environment.
- **Sony WH-1000XM5**: Another excellent choice for noise-canceling headphones with high-quality sound.
- **Apple AirPods Pro**: Ideal for those who prefer compact, in-ear noise-canceling headphones.

Desk Organization Tools

- **Cable Management Clips**: Keep your workspace tidy by organizing cables and cords.
- **Standing Desks**: Adjustable desks that allow you to switch between sitting and standing for improved posture and focus.
- **Minimalist Desk Lamps**: Lighting with adjustable brightness to reduce eye strain and enhance focus.

7. Tools for Tracking Progress and Accountability

Tracking your focus and productivity helps you stay accountable and make continuous improvements.

Habit Tracking Apps

- **Habitica**: Turns habit-building into a game, rewarding you for completing tasks and maintaining focus.
- **Streaks**: A simple habit tracker that motivates you to keep streaks going by completing daily tasks.
- **Loop Habit Tracker**: A free, open-source app for tracking habits and visualizing progress over time.

Focus Trackers

- **RescueTime**: Monitors how you spend your time on devices, providing insights into where you can improve focus.
- **Toggl Track**: A time-tracking tool that helps you understand how long tasks take and optimize your schedule.
- **Clockify**: A free time tracker for individuals and teams to monitor productivity.

8. Books and Educational Resources on Focus

Reading about focus and productivity can provide valuable insights and inspiration.

Books

- *Deep Work* by Cal Newport: A foundational book on cultivating focus in a distracted world.
- *Atomic Habits* by James Clear: Explores how small, consistent changes can build powerful habits, including focus.
- *The Power of Now* by Eckhart Tolle: A guide to mindfulness and staying present in the moment.

Online Resources

- **TED Talks on Focus and Productivity**: Inspiring talks by experts in time management and concentration.
- **The Focus Course by Shawn Blanc**: A premium course designed to help you master focus through structured training.

Conclusion

This list of tools, apps, and resources is designed to provide you with everything you need to build, sustain, and enhance your focus. Whether you're looking to eliminate distractions, manage your time better, or create an environment conducive to deep work, these recommendations offer practical solutions for every aspect of focus improvement. Experiment with different tools and strategies to find what works best for you, and remember that maintaining focus is an ongoing journey of refinement and adaptation.

<u>Message from the Author:</u>

I hope you enjoyed this book, I love astrology and knew there was not a book such as this out on the shelf. I love metaphysical items as well. Please check out my other books:

-Life of Government Benefits

-My life of Hell

-My life with Hydrocephalus

-Red Sky

-World Domination:Woman's rule

-World Domination:Woman's Rule 2: The War

-Life and Banishment of Apophis: book 1

-The Kidney Friendly Diet

-The Ultimate Hemp Cookbook

-Creating a Dispensary(legally)

-Cleanliness throughout life: the importance of showering from childhood to adulthood.

-Strong Roots: The Risks of Overcoddling children

-Hemp Horoscopes: Cosmic Insights and Earthly Healing

- Celestial Hemp Navigating the Zodiac: Through the Green Cosmos

-Astrological Hemp: Aligning The Stars with Earth's Ancient Herb

-The Astrological Guide to Hemp: Stars, Signs, and Sacred Leaves

-Green Growth: Innovative Marketing Strategies for your Hemp Products and Dispensary

-Cosmic Cannabis

-Astrological Munchies

-Henry The Hemp

-Zodiacal Roots: The Astrological Soul Of Hemp

- **Green Constellations: Intersection of Hemp and Zodiac**

-Hemp in The Houses: An astrological Adventure Through The Cannabis Galaxy

-Galactic Ganja Guide

Heavenly Hemp

Zodiac Leaves

Doctor Who Astrology

Cannastrology

Stellar Satvias and Cosmic Indicas

Celestial Cannabis: A Zodiac Journey

AstroHerbology: The Sky and The Soil: Volume 1

AstroHerbology:Celestial Cannabis:Volume 2

Cosmic Cannabis Cultivation

The Starry Guide to Herbal Harmony: Volume 1

The Starry Guide to Herbal Harmony: Cannabis Universe: Volume 2

Yugioh Astrology: Astrological Guide to Deck, Duels and more

Nightmare Mansion: Echoes of The Abyss

Nightmare Mansion 2: Legacy of Shadows

Nightmare Mansion 3: Shadows of the Forgotten

Nightmare Mansion 4: Echoes of the Damned

The Life and Banishment of Apophis: Book 2

Nightmare Mansion: Halls of Despair

Healing with Herb: Cannabis and Hydrocephalus

Planetary Pot: Aligning with Astrological Herbs: Volume 1

Fast Track to Freedom: 30 Days to Financial Independence Using AI, Assets, and Agile Hustles

Cosmic Hemp Pathways

How to Become Financially Free in 30 Days: 10,000 Paths to Prosperity

Zodiacal Herbage: Astrological Insights: Volume 1

Nightmare Mansion: Whispers in the Walls
The Daleks Invade Atlantis
Henry the hemp and Hydrocephalus

10X The Kidney Friendly Diet
Cannabis Universe: Adult coloring book
Hemp Astrology: The Healing Power of the Stars
Zodiacal Herbage: Astrological Insights: Cannabis Universe: Volume 2
<u>Planetary Pot: Aligning with Astrological Herbs: Cannabis Universes: Volume 2</u>
Doctor Who Meets the Replicators and SG-1: The Ultimate Battle for Survival
Nightmare Mansion: Curse of the Blood Moon
<u>The Celestial Stoner: A Guide to the Zodiac</u>
Cosmic Pleasures: Sex Toy Astrology for Every Sign
Hydrocephalus Astrology: Navigating the Stars and Healing Waters
Lapis and the Mischievous Chocolate Bar

Celestial Positions: Sexual Astrology for Every Sign
Apophis's Shadow Work Journal: : A Journey of Self-Discovery and Healing
Kinky Cosmos: Sexual Kink Astrology for Every Sign
Digital Cosmos: The Astrological Digimon Compendium
Stellar Seeds: The Cosmic Guide to Growing with Astrology
Apophis's Daily Gratitude Journal

Cat Astrology: Feline Mysteries of the Cosmos
The Cosmic Kama Sutra: An Astrological Guide to Sexual Positions
Unleash Your Potential: A Guided Journal Powered by AI Insights
Whispers of the Enchanted Grove

Cosmic Pleasures: An Astrological Guide to Sexual Kinks

369, 12 Manifestation Journal

Whisper of the nocturne journal(blank journal for writing or drawing)

The Boogey Book

Locked In Reflection: A Chastity Journey Through Locktober

Generating Wealth Quickly:

How to Generate $100,000 in 24 Hours

Star Magic: Harness the Power of the Universe

The Flatulence Chronicles: A Fart Journal for Self-Discovery

The Doctor and The Death Moth

Seize the Day: A Personal Seizure Tracking Journal

The Ultimate Boogeyman Safari: A Journey into the Boogie World and Beyond

Whispers of Samhain: 1,000 Spells of Love, Luck, and Lunar Magic: Samhain Spell Book

Apophis's guides:

Witch's Spellbook Crafting Guide for Halloween

<u>Frost & Flame: The Enchanted Yule Grimoire of 1000 Winter Spells</u>

<u>The Ultimate Boogey Goo Guide & Spooky Activities for Halloween Fun</u>

Harmony of the Scales: A Libra's Spellcraft for Balance and Beauty

The Enchanted Advent: 36 Days of Christmas Wonders

Nightmare Mansion: The Labyrinth of Screams

Harvest of Enchantment: 1,000 Spells of Gratitude, Love, and Fortune for Thanksgiving

The Boogey Chronicles: A Journal of Nightly Encounters and Shadowy Secrets

The 12 Days of Financial Freedom: A Step-by-Step Christmas Countdown to Transform Your Finances

Sigil of the Eternal Spiral Blank Journal

A Christmas Feast: Timeless Recipes for Every Meal

Holiday Stress-Free Solutions: A Survival Guide to Thriving During the Festive Season

Yu-Gi-Oh! Holiday Gifting Mastery: The Ultimate Guide for Fans and Newcomers Alike

Holiday Harmony: A Hydrocephalus Survival Guide for the Festive Season

Celestial Craft: The Witch's Almanac for 2025 – A Cosmic Guide to Manifestations, Moons, and Mystical Events

Doctor Who: The Toymaker's Winter Wonderland

Tulsa King Unveiled: A Thrilling Guide to Stallone's Mafia Masterpiece

Pendulum Craft: A Complete Guide to Crafting and Using Personalized Divination Tools

Nightmare Mansion: Santa's Eternal Eve

Starlight Noel: A Cosmic Journey through Christmas Mysteries

The Dark Architect: Unlocking the Blueprint of Existence

Surviving the Embrace: The Ultimate Guide to Encounters with The Hugging Molly

The Enchanted Codex: Secrets of the Craft for Witches, Wiccans, and Pagans

Harvest of Gratitude: A Complete Thanksgiving Guide

Yuletide Essentials: A Complete Guide to an Authentic and Magical Christmas

Celestial Smokes: A Cosmic Guide to Cigars and Astrology

Living in Balance: A Comprehensive Survival Guide to Thriving with Diabetes Insipidus

Cosmic Symbiosis: The Venom Zodiac Chronicles

The Cursed Paw of Ambition

Cosmic Symbiosis: The Astrological Venom Journal

Celestial Wonders Unfold: A Stargazer's Guide to the Cosmos (2024-2029)

The Ultimate Black Friday Prepper's Guide: Mastering Shopping Strategies and Savings

Cosmic Sales: The Astrological Guide to Black Friday Shopping

Legends of the Corn Mother and Other Harvest Myths

Whispers of the Harvest: The Corn Mother's Journal

The Evergreen Spellbook

The Doctor Meets the Boogeyman

The White Witch of Rose Hall's SpellBook

The Gingerbread Golem's Shadow: A Study in Sweet Darkness

The Gingerbread Golem Codex: An Academic Exploration of Sweet Myths

The Gingerbread Golem Grimoire: Sweet Magicks and Spells for the Festive Witch

The Curse of the Gingerbread Golem

10-minute Christmas Crafts for kids

<u>Christmas Crisis Solutions: The Ultimate Last-Minute Survival Guide</u>

Gingerbread Golem Recipes: Holiday Treats with a Magical Twist

The Infinite Key: Unlocking Mystical Secrets of the Ages

Enchanted Yule: A Wiccan and Pagan Guide to a Magical and Memorable Season

Dinosaurs of Power: Unlocking Ancient Magick

Astro-Dinos: The Cosmic Guide to Prehistoric Wisdom

Gallifrey's Yule Logs: A Festive Doctor Who Cookbook

The Dino Grimoire: Secrets of Prehistoric Magick

The Gift They Never Knew They Needed

The Gingerbread Golem's Culinary Alchemy: Enchanting Recipes for a Sweetly Dark Feast

A Time Lord Christmas: Holiday Adventures with the Doctor

Krampusproofing Your Home: Defensive Strategies for Yule

Silent Frights: A Collection of Christmas Creepypastas to Chill Your Bones

Santa Raptor's Jolly Carnage: A Dino-Claus Christmas Tale

If you want solar for your home go here: https://www.harborso-lar.live/apophisenterprises/

Get Some Tarot cards: https://www.makeplayingcards.com/sell/apophis-occult-shop

Get   some   shirts: https://www.bonfire.com/store/apophis-shirt-emporium/

Instagrams:
@apophis_enterprises,
@apophisbookemporium,
@apophisscardshop
Twitter: @apophisenterpr1
Tiktok:@apophisenterprise
Youtube: @sg1fan23477, @FiresideRetreatKingdom
Hive: @sg1fan23477
CheeLee: @SG1fan23477

Podcast: Apophis Chat Zone: https://open.spotify.com/show/
5zXbrCLEV2xzCp8ybrfHsk?si=fb4d4fdbdce44dec

Newsletter: https://apophiss-newsletter-27c897.beehiiv.com/

If you want to support me or see posts of other projects that I have come over to: **buymeacoffee.com/mpetchinskg**
I post there daily several times a day

Get your Dinowicca or Christmas themed digital products, especially Santa Raptor songs and other musics. Here: **https://sg1fan23477.gumroad.com**

Apophis Yuletide Digital has not only digital Christmas items, but it will have all things with Dinowicca as well as other Digital products.